I AM

THE STATEMENTS OF JESUS

JOHN PENNYLEGION

White Blackbird
BOOKS

John Pennylegion's use of Jesus' "I am" statements to endear our hearts to the identity of the Savior also help us know how dear we are to him. If he is our bread, then we are beloved children provided food from heaven. If he is our Good Shepherd, then we are precious sheep for whom he gives his life. When we honestly ask, "Who Jesus is?", we discover his "I am" statements help every child of God really know whose I am and who I am.
Bryan Chapell
Pastor
Author, *Holiness by Grace*

Jesus Christ has worked into John Pennylegion all the qualities you want in a really fine preacher. He is studious and careful, thoughtful and honest, earnest and sincere, approachable and clear. In these studies from John's gospel, he helps us to know and love Jesus better and to center our identity in following him. It is a genuine pleasure to commend this book to you!
C. John ("Jack") Collins, PhD
Professor of Old Testament, Covenant Theological Seminary

Writing with the tenderness of a pastor who loves Jesus,

and the conviction of one who loves people, John Pennylegion's *I Am* is a true gift to us all. As he helpfully unpacks Jesus' "I am" statements, Pennylegion invites you into the wonder and freedom of knowing Jesus. It is as nourishing as it is enjoyable to read, and it is a book I am sure I will continue to return to with joy.

Charles Johnson
Pastor

We live in a cultural moment when proclaiming your own sense of self-identity is considered a basic right. Yet, ironically, we tend to not afford Jesus this same basic right. But what if we did? What if we simply let Jesus describe himself? What if we let Jesus state who he thought he was and what he was all about? This is precisely what we see him doing in the famous "I am" statements that this book explores. With the familiarity of one who knows and walks with Jesus, Pastor John Pennylegion opens up the meaning of these statements. Displaying both depth of insight as well as practical application Pennylegion encourages us to let our understanding of Jesus be reshaped by Jesus' understanding of himself.

Travis Scott
Pastor
Author, *Faithful Doubt: Habakkuk.*

How would you describe yourself to others? What if you

could only pick only seven statements to do it? What would you want them to know—not about what you have done, but about who you are. Likewise, what if we got to know Jesus, not by talking about him, but by listening to how he describes himself? That is what John Pennylegion unpacks for us in his new devotional book, taking us through the seven "I Am" statements found in the gospel of John. We see Jesus revealing who he is, bit by bit—Bread, Light, Door and so. But it is not enough to simply read each statement on its own. Pennylegion helps us understand each one in their cultural and scriptural contexts. What we find is that Jesus is far more than we could ever hope for. And he is here for us.

Chris Hutchinson

Pastor

Author, *Rediscovering Humility: Why the Way Up Is Down*

My friend John Pennylegion's reflections on the seven "I am" statements of Jesus in the gospel of John provide a model for us in how to read Scripture devotionally. The result is an edifying exposition of the person of Christ that will serve as both an encouragement for Christians and an excellent resource to give to those exploring Christianity.

Gavin Ortlund

Pastor

Author, *Finding the Right Hills to Die On: The Case for Theological Triage*

In this book, we get a clearer view of who Jesus claims to be. John Pennylegion opens up the "I Am" statements of Jesus in a way that is understandable, encouraging, and stokes a deeper love for Jesus. Highly relevant and practical, this book will center your mind's attention and your heart's affection on who Jesus is and what that means for your life.

Michael Novak
Pastor

Be drawn to worship Christ as you're reminded of—or discover for the first time—who Jesus is. Pennylegion's *I Am* offers a clear, relatable, and refreshing look at the truth of who Jesus is. Knowing who Christ is—and who we are not—is foundational to developing a biblical worldview, which is vital to fulfilling God's call to be salt and light in today's world.

Dr. Kelly Haer
Executive Director, Boone Center for the Family, Pepperdine University

Much like he is as a peer and a friend, John Pennylegion remains true to himself as he conveys biblical truths with a Christlike kindness that challenges the mind while softening the heart. His presentation of who Jesus is, in light of who we are, cultivates an uncomfortable yet beautifully intimate relationship with a God who is accessible to his people. Readers will find a deeper knowledge of both self and Christ. This will ultimately lead to a journey of uncovering the power of who God is, what he has done for his people, and why his "I Am" statements *matter.*

Louise Adams
MA in Counseling, PLPC

To Kat, Laine, Mead, and Cole—

*Your love, grace, and care comfort
my heart and are a balm to my soul.*

CONTENTS

WHO DO YOU SAY HE IS?

Jesus once asked his disciples, *"Who do people say that I am?"* (Mark 8:27). The disciples had heard many possibilities of who their teacher was: *"John the Baptist; and others say, Elijah; and others, one of the prophets"* (Mark 8:28). Evidently in the area around first-century Jerusalem, there were a variety of opinions about who this carpenter was. Since that moment in Mark 8 (cf. Matt. 16:13ff), people have been attempting to identify who Jesus is. Some of the claims have been true, while others are far from the truth. Answering questions about Jesus' identity is one of the most important things we can do. Millions and millions of people have centered their faith around the belief that Jesus is the foundation, reason, and the motivation for life.

Who do you say he is?

Before we lean on our own understanding or adopt

what others have said, we must consider what Jesus said about himself.

In the gospel of John, Jesus makes seven statements that specifically focus on his identity. These are the seven "I am" statements. Of course, many of Jesus' claims that don't include the words, "I am" give insight into who he was. For instance, Jesus made claims about the Old Testament expectation concerning the "Son of Man" (cf. Matt. 8:20, 9:6; Mark 9:31, 10:45; Luke 5:24, 9:22; John 1:51, 3:13, etc.). He spoke as one who fulfills the Old Testament prophecies concerning the Messiah (cf. Matt. 26:56; Luke 4:21, 22:37; etc.). He spoke and acted as God incarnate (cf. Matt 9:2, 9:5; John 8:58; etc.), etc. These help to shape our understanding of Jesus' identity. It would take a great deal of well-spent time to consider these various identifiers. However, the focus of this book will be the seven metaphors in John that are preceded by the phrase, "I am."

Theologians point out that what makes these state-ments unique is the Greek, *ego eimi,* which we translate as "I am." The structure of these statements helps us to understand them as being emphatic as well as speaking of Jesus' divinity.[1] John 8:58 says: *"Truly, truly, I say to you, before Abraham was, I am."* While this statement is similar to the other seven, the construction of the clause differs. In John 8, Jesus does not follow "I am" with a metaphor to describe who is or what he does. Instead, John 8:58 leaves the "I am" as a statement on its own, one of divinity and eternality.[2] Of course this is significant, but the difference leads us to take the seven statements together and to treat John 8 on its own. Our focus will be on the seven "I am" statements that aren't in John 8.

As we consider these words of Jesus, we'll see that each reveals a different aspect of who he is. It shouldn't surprise us that Jesus was a multifaceted person.

That's true for all of us as people. If you were to list all the ways that you describe yourself and communicate who you are, you would come up with many adjectives. For example—I'm a Christian, husband, father, pastor, American, Canadian, former college athlete, a once-upon-a-time suburban gardener, a cyclist, and much more. We often choose the way we describe ourselves based on context. We consider how our experience might be helpful to the situation we're in or what our conversation partner is needing to know.

Before going any further, it is important to say that I'm not advocating for the way many in our culture seemingly put on and put off identity markers at will. I can't stop being a former college athlete or a father— these are part of who I am. However, they are not the fullness, or even the foundation, of who I am. For Christians, the most important part of our identity is that we are followers of Christ. This central aspect to who we are dictates how we appropriate all the other descriptors we employ. Everything about who we are and how we live flows out of our identity as being a follower of Jesus. While this is the truest part of who we are, we still have other parts of us that communicate different aspects of our experience that are unique to us. This is no different for Jesus. Hence, seven different statements that speak about different aspects of who Jesus is and what he came to do.

This book originated from the first sermon series I did when I came to be the pastor of Christ the King Presbyterian Church in Roanoke, Virginia. I began my preaching ministry at CTK with these sayings because I believed them to be foundational to our following of Jesus.

Each time I have read these passages I've seen the beauty of Jesus and been confronted with my need to follow him. I hope that as you read these adapted sermons, that you too will see more of Jesus and seek to follow him more faithfully.

While I wrote this with Christians in mind, my hope is that those who have been curious about Jesus, flirted with Christianity, or have turned away from the Church, would benefit from this work as well. No single person has influenced the world more than Jesus. Thus, it is worth our time and energy to seriously consider what he said.

Who do you say he is?

BREAD FOR THE HUNGRY

John 6:35–51

Jesus said to them, "I am the bread of life;
whoever comes to me shall not hunger,
and whoever believes in me shall never thirst."

There was a season in the life of my family where once a week after dinner, my kids and I would congregate on the couch. They had brushed their teeth and were in their pajamas. Before they headed off to bed, we would watch the reality cooking show "Master Chef." We loved seeing amateur chefs prepare amazing dishes. Inevitably, somewhere on the couch, from the bottom of their bellies, I would hear a low rumble: "Mmmmm." Forget that they were full from dinner or that they couldn't taste, touch, or even smell the creations—the very sight of these dishes made my kids want them. They could find room in their stomachs for a slice of cake or a bite of chicken. Whether we eat it or just see it prepared, an incredible meal creates a hunger in us.

I imagine this is what the crowds and the Jews who surrounded Jesus were experiencing. The context of John 6 is that Jesus miraculously fed five thousand people with five loaves of bread and two fish. A day later, the crowd had caught up to him, and the Jews were looking for him. They had not just heard about a miracle. They experienced it firsthand. They had touched, tasted, and eaten their full, and now the very sight of Jesus made them hunger for more. They came to the chef who had been responsible for an incredible meal, and they asked him to do it again. In verse 34, after Jesus had told them that there was a true bread that comes from God, the people said to him, *"Sir, give us this bread always."*

In response to their request, Jesus could have given them more food, bread, or fish. He could have taken water from the lake and made it into wine, but that's not what he did. Instead of giving them another meal, Jesus clarified what they had actually tasted and touched, what they were actually craving.

Craving

Jesus said, *"I am the bread of life; whoever comes to me shall not hunger, and whoever believes in me shall never thirst"*

(John 6:35). Jesus described himself as the bread of life, the one who ends hunger and thirst. By declaring himself to be the bread of life, Jesus was not saying that our physical hunger will be completely assuaged. We know that no matter the meal, our bodies will need sustenance again. Even after Thanksgiving dinner when we indulge in great amounts of food, four, eight, or twenty-four hours later, we will be hungry again. That's not the type of hunger that Jesus is satisfying. By offering himself as the bread of life, Jesus declares that he is the satisfier of our spiritual, emotional, and relational cravings.

Jesus' promise of satisfying our craving is significant because we frequently look to be filled with things that promise satisfaction but leave us hungry. Why do we remain in a manipulative relationship? Because we have an appetite for love, even dysfunctional love. Why do we bury ourselves in our work? One of the reasons is because we have a hunger for approval, even false approval. Why do we let our convictions slide? Because to hold to them might mean rejection, and we thirst for acceptance, even if it's conditional. We deal with our hunger pangs by filling ourselves with things that look appealing. We try to satisfy our cravings with things that are enticing. However, like that giant meal, when we try to satisfy our deepest cravings and hungers with something or someone other than Jesus, we are left feeling bloated and hungry again.

This isn't new to the twenty-first century. The

prophet Isaiah, writing in the eighth century BC, spoke the word of the Lord. He said in Isaiah 55:1–2a:

> *Come, everyone who thirsts, come to the waters; and he who has no money, come, buy and eat! Come, buy wine and milk without money and without price. Why do you spend your money for that which is not bread, and your labor for that which does not satisfy?*

Through the prophet, God asks, "Why are you content with the approval of men, the conditional love of those who don't actually love us, the acceptance of those who only accept us for a moment?" The passage goes on. In verses 2b–3 we read, *"Listen diligently to me, and eat what is good, and delight yourselves in rich food. Incline your ear, and come to me...."* Thousands of years before Jesus fed those five thousand people, the prophet announced that we are to find our satisfaction not in this world but in someone who would satisfy our cravings.

Jesus now says, "I am that food. You tasted the bread I gave you, now taste of me. You will never hunger." Jesus is the one who comes from heaven, and he offers himself. He is clarifying that he is the one we are craving.

You would think that having seen what they had seen, having tasted what they had tasted, and having heard Jesus' clarification, the people would rejoice. But that's not what they do. Instead of receiving what had been offered with joy, they complained.

Complaining

In verses 41–42 we're told, *"The Jews grumbled about him, because he said, 'I am the bread that came down from heaven.' They said, 'Is not this Jesus, the son of Joseph, whose father and mother we know? How does he now say, 'I have come down from heaven'?"* Their grumbling reflected a distortion in what they had seen and who they were talking to. They didn't want to satisfy their ultimate hungers, only their immediate ones. Jesus offered them something that lasts, yet they were content with what is fleeting. They were wanting the magical, the mysterious, and the miraculous. But Jesus offered them something better than the miraculous. He offered the miracle worker himself. The crowd had experienced something good, and they were so transfixed that when something better was offered, they couldn't comprehend it. They were like the child who rejects the filet mignon and instead devours the microwaved hotdog. Though the hotdog might satisfy their momentary hunger, there is something far more delicious before them. The people grumbled and complained instead of seeing what was being offered.

The response of the crowd and the Jews shouldn't surprise us. It was what God's people had done time and time again. In his prelude to his statement, manna in the wilderness was brought up. The people had said to Jesus, *"Our fathers ate the manna in the wilderness"* (John 6:31).

It is true that God had provided manna for their fathers, but they were only telling a portion of the story.

Prior to God's giving manna, the people grumbled. They said in Exodus 16:3, *"Would that we had died by the hand of the LORD in the land of Egypt... for you have brought us out into this wilderness to kill this whole assembly with hunger."* This statement is incredibly sad because it came from those who had seen God's miraculous works and experienced his grace. God had rescued them from Egypt, he warred against Pharaoh, he defeated Egypt's gods, and he led his people through the sea. Having experienced God's rescue, the people responded to his great works by grumbling. They wanted more. So God graciously gave them manna.

Yet that wasn't enough. The people had food, but they didn't have water, so they grumbled again. Graciously, God gave them water. Yet the grumbling did not end. Later in Numbers 11:4b–6, the people had food and drink, and they said, *"Oh that we had meat to eat! We remember the fish we ate in Egypt that cost nothing, the cucumbers, the melons, the leeks, the onions, and the garlic. But now our strength is dried up, and there is nothing at all but this manna to look at."* They grumbled when they didn't have food, when they didn't have drink, and when they didn't have meat.

And the people who heard Jesus' words imitated their fathers and grumbled at Jesus' claim *"I am the bread that came down from heaven"* (John 6:41).

We are not much different than Israel in the wilderness or the Jewish people of Jesus' day. We grumble too. If you're reading this and are a Christian, you're probably not complaining because of who Jesus says he is. We don't grumble at the bread provided that first day of belief. We grumble at the provision that follows. We complain because we don't have the talents we want. We grumble because we don't have the children we think we deserve. We bemoan not having the job we think we've earned. We gripe because we don't have the spouse we've hoped for. We complain. And in our grumbling, we show that we too have a distorted view of Jesus. Our view says he is the bread of life for our salvation, but we need more than that bread for today.

Maybe you're reading this and you're not a Christian. Your complaint is going to be different. Maybe you look at the world, the disarray and anger, the angst and disillusionment, and you're looking for an answer, and what you hear from the church is that the thing you're looking for is Jesus. So maybe you grumble, "Jesus! Really? That's it? No seven steps to a better life? No virtue training? A man who lived thousands of years ago? That seems too simple."

Your complaints and your questions aren't new. The Jews disbelieved, and they grumbled at Jesus' words because they thought they knew what they needed to satisfy their cravings. Maybe that's why you complain as well. We know we have longings, unmet desires, and questions. We expect to solve these problems with the newest fad, a renewed view of self, or that book that promises a way to a better life.

You know what I'm talking about. It's the cream that

says you'll look younger, the pill that promises you'll be healthier, etc., etc. But we keep looking for the next thing because the old thing, that was once the next thing, has left us hungry. What we need is for our souls to be satisfied; what we desire is life. That's what Jesus offers when he offers himself.

His Offer

In verses 43, 47–51 Jesus says:

> Do not grumble among yourselves.... Truly, truly, I say to you, whoever believes has eternal life. I am the bread of life. Your fathers ate the manna in the wilderness, and they died. This is the bread that comes down from heaven, so that one may eat of it and not die. I am the living bread that came down from heaven. If anyone eats of this bread, he will live forever. And the bread that I will give for the life of the world is my flesh.

Jesus is about more than simply getting us through the day or momentary satisfaction. He is concerned about eternality.[1]

Remember I have previously mentioned Isaiah 55. I stopped at the beginning of verse 3. The prophet's words continue. God invites his people to come, eat and drink, and then he says, "hear, that your soul may live...." That your soul may live—not that your bellies would be full for a moment or that you would have enjoyment for a day, but that you would live for eternity. This is what Jesus was telling the crowds and what he is telling us. Though our throats will thirst, we will be quenched; though we will hunger, we will be filled full. There is nothing in this world that can do this. Whatever we consume, be it food or drink, good works or moral behavior—they will all leave us grasping for more. We are longing for something not of this world. Saint Augustine once argued that the whole of the Christian life is a holy longing in which we are to sever our longings for the things of this world.[2]

The experiences and cravings that are unsatisfied in this world point to our need for something not of this world, something of heaven. Jesus said that he is the bread that came down from heaven (John 6:38). And when he was asked, *"What must we do, to be doing the work of God"?* (John 6:28), Jesus responded, *"This is the work of God, that you believe in him whom he has sent"* (John 6:29). Believe in Jesus who, by his grace, takes our longings and gives us life. He takes our grumbling and turns it into gratitude. He takes our resignation to death and raises us up for eternity.

2

LIVING BY THE LIGHT

John 8:12

*Again Jesus spoke to them, saying, "I am the light
of the world. Whoever follows me will not
walk in darkness, but will have the light of life."*

I lived my entire pre-college life in a split-level home.
For those who do not know what a split-level house
is, when you come in the front door, you stand on a
landing and there are stairs leading upstairs and another
set of stairs heading down. The kitchen, dining room,
and bedrooms were all upstairs. Downstairs was where
we played—ping pong, movies, and television. As I
descended the first flight of stairs and stood on the
landing looking down, there were times when I froze in

fear. The fear often overwhelmed me at night because above me was a room filled with light, but below me was only the dark. There I stood, unable to reach the light switch. I would stand on my tippy toes and reach as best as I could, but I couldn't turn the light on. Standing at the top of the stairs looking down into the darkness, I was so afraid.

Darkness can be a scary place for young children. Behind closet doors, under beds, and around corners— our imagination starts to run wild. Who knows what might be lurking?

The darkness isn't only a scary place for children but also for adults. It's not the literal darkness that scares us. It's the darkness that fills our world and surrounds us. People ask, "What is happening to our world? What is going on in our city and our country?" We see senseless violence, hear of hostility, and have a growing concern over the future. It can feel like we are being over-whelmed by a shroud darkness that fills us with worry and fear.

Standing with fear at the top of the stairs, I knew what was below. At the bottom of the stairs was a hallway that ended in the family room. I knew that at the entrance to the family room was a table and sitting on the table was a lamp. If I could muster up the courage to walk into the dark and run down the hall to the lamp, I knew I would be okay. And I was.

As soon as the lamp clicked on and the light shined into the room, my fear fled as quickly as the darkness did. The light gave me assurance that I didn't need to fear. The darkness wasn't as powerful as I perceived it to be. This is not only true of the darkness that fills our basements but also the darkness in our world. We know this to be true not because we have mustered up the courage to go looking for the lamp that will overwhelm the darkness but because the light has already come. This light comes not from ourselves, but from God. A light has erupted in the midst of the darkness of our world and that light is Jesus. As the light, Jesus tells us that he brings life.

The Light That Brings Life

Jesus' statement of who he is has implications for what he does. Not only is he the light that breaks into the darkness, but he says that those who follow him *"will have the light of life"* (John 8:12). This clearly implies that we are in need of life.

The imagery of light producing life is easy for us to understand. We know that the seeds we plant in the ground will lie dormant until the right conditions come together to bring forth life, and one of these factors is light. It doesn't matter how much water we shower them with or the amount of fertilizer we put in the ground. Without light, the seed will not sprout. Life will never come apart from the light.

This is where the analogy breaks down. We are not simply lying dormant waiting for the right environmental factors. The Bible tells us that in our sin, we are spiritually dead (cf. Eph. 2:1, 5; Col. 2:13). Not comatose, not dormant—dead. As a result of this, we need something from outside of us to overtake the deadness and breathe life into us. That's what Jesus says he does. Forget for a moment about the darkness in the world. Jesus comes into the darkness of our hearts, and because of his love for us, he shines life-giving light into us.

When I lived in St. Louis, I had a sizable vegetable garden. After a year or two, I started planting from seeds and began the growing indoors. I started lettuce, tomatoes, and even apple trees inside away from the sun. I used artificial lights.

But we can't do that with our lives. We can try artificial lights—like giving to charity, loving our spouse, being kind to the needy, volunteering, and a whole host of things that we think will give us life. While these are good, they are unable to produce life. They are not the true light. That is what Jesus is called in 1 John 2:8 *"the true light...."* Jesus is the giver of life, the defeater of darkness, and the true light that brings salvation.

The Light for the Way

What is beautiful about what Jesus accomplishes is that he is not done with us after he gives us life. He does not bring light and then recede to let us go any way that we like. As he brings life, he also lights the way for how we are to live. In verse 12, he says, *"Whoever follows me will not walk in darkness."* This theme of a light that guides our way is a common biblical idea. Throughout scripture, God's directing of his people is often described as light.

After God had delivered his people out of Egypt and led them into the wilderness, he directed them with a pillar of cloud by day and *"by night a pillar of fire to give them light"* (Exod. 13:21). When the psalmist spoke of God's law, he wrote, *"Your word is a lamp to my feet and a light to my path"* (Ps. 119:105). Later in his life, the Apostle John said that to *"walk in the light"* is to have fellowship with Christ and his church (1 John 1:6–7). There are many other places we could turn to emphasize this: Proverbs, the prophets, and other places in the New Testament. We need Jesus' light not just for new life but also along the path of life.

We need this direction because we are prone to return to the darkness. Every one of us has a proclivity towards sin and temptation. We have places in our hearts and minds that we hold onto, and instead of resisting the darkness and exposing those places to the light, we keep them in the dark.

We convince ourselves that they will bring life. But that is not the way of Christ. Jesus has shined into the darkness not so we would put aside the light, but that we would live by it. This is what the Christian life is to look like—following Jesus wherever he would lead. That is why John says, *"If we say we have fellowship with him while we walk in the darkness, we lie and do not practice the truth"* (1 John 1:6). Though we may be prone to return to the dark, for those who have experienced Christ's shining light, our lives are to be marked by following him.

We resist the creeping darkness and pursue lives that follow him by being people of his Word. Since God's Word is to be understood as *"a light to my path"* (Ps. 119:105), we need to be people who know God's Word, love it, and live by it. In order to orient our lives around God's Word, we need to read it diligently.

Now before you skip to the next section because "you've heard this before," let me acknowledge that this can feel like just another thing to do. Yet, if you wanted to lead a healthy life, you would make time for exercise, make healthy meals, pay attention to how much rest you get, and much more. You would do these things because you value the outcome that they will bring.

God's word is no different. If walking in the light is important, and it is, it's imperative we make time for it. This doesn't mean you have to be a Bible scholar. You don't need to know Greek or Hebrew or have a functional understanding of hermeneutical theories.

All you need is a Bible and time. When do you have time? When are you alone? Driving to work? Doing the laundry? Cutting the grass? You could spend those times listening to the Word of God. Use the time you already have to be ministered to by the light of God's Word.

The Light We Reflect

As we go along the way, following the light, we will be reflectors of it. In Matthew 5–7, Jesus gave his Sermon on the Mount. This is a sermon that was spoken to his disciples about what life in his kingdom is to look like. Jesus said:

> *You are the light of the world. A city set on a hill cannot be hidden. Nor do people light a lamp and put it under a basket, but on a stand, and it gives light to all in the house. In the same way, let your light shine before others, so that they may see your good works and give glory to your Father who is in heaven.* (Matt. 5:14–16)

This is identity language. When Jesus spoke of himself, he said, *"I am the light of the world."* In Matthew 5, he said of his disciples, *"You are the light of the world."* Jesus places on us the same name that he embraced for himself. That means that we are no longer marked by darkness, but we are now identified as light.

I played baseball at Lander University. My coach didn't only speak to us about the nuances of baseball, but he also gave us a vision for what it meant to be a member of the Lander baseball team. He called this vision The Lander Way, a particular way of playing the game. We sprinted on and off the field, we ran out every ground ball, and we played hard all the time. But this vision wasn't limited only to baseball. It was to encompass other areas of our lives—how we presented ourselves in the classroom, how we spoke to our professors, and how we interacted in the community. Because we were members of the Lander baseball team, we now represented it all the time. Whether we had our jersey on or not, wherever we went, we went with this identity. We went as representatives of the team.

This is not only for those of us who played for Coach Stroupe at Lander University. In a far more significant way, this is true of followers of Jesus. As those who have been brought out of the dark, we have a new identity, and because of this identity we are now Jesus' ambassadors of light. We take this identity with us everywhere we go.

This means that we now live in response to his light by living for others. We live so others may see our *"good works and give glory to [our] Father who is in heaven"* (Matt. 5:16). Through our lives and words, we point to the Father who sent his Son, the Light, so that the nations would come out of the darkness.

The Light that Shines Forever

I'm happy to say that I no longer freeze with fear at the top of the stairs when the lights are off. But when my children were younger, I was regularly reminded of the fear that darkness can bring. Occasionally my children would express worry and concern over the darkness that filled their rooms as they went to bed.

My wife quickly got each of them a nightlight. Every night when we put them to bed, we turned on this tiny little light. It's amazing how much comfort came from such a small device. The little bit of light that shone from that bulb rid them of their fear so they could sleep in peace.

We know that over time the bulb will burn out, the light will be extinguished, and darkness will fill the room again. I imagine that when Jesus was nailed to the cross, crucified, dead, and buried, that his enemies were convinced that this light had been snuffed out. That his light was momentary. Perhaps even his disciples thought that as well.

However, they would soon realize that the darkness had not overcome him (John 1:5). Jesus' residing in the grave was like a dimmer—the light had gone low only to burn brighter in his resurrection. For no amount of darkness could cover this light. His light shines forever.

In Revelation 21:22–25, we are given an incredible picture of the new heavens and the new earth. John describes it like this:

> *And I saw no temple in the city, for its temple is the Lord God the Almighty and the Lamb. And the city has no need of sun or moon to shine on it, for the glory of God gives it light, and its lamp is the Lamb. By its light will the nations walk, and the kings of the of the earth will bring their glory into it, and its gates will never be shut by day—and there will be no night there.*

The light of Christ continues forever, and his brightness does not grow dim over time. There is a day coming when all things will be made right. There will be no more darkness and no more night because Christ's glory will burn bright.

As we wait for that day, we need not fear the darkness because we have been made alive by the light.

3

THE DOOR

John 10:1–10

So Jesus again said to them, "Truly, truly, I say
to you, I am the door of the sheep....
I am the door. If anyone enters by me, he will be
saved and will go in and out and find pasture."

Hiking is popular in Southwest Virginia. Shortly after my family and I moved to Roanoke, we set out on our first hike. We drove into the Jefferson National Forest and embarked on Roaring Run Falls. Bridges, trees, the river, and the falls—it was beautiful.

Since then, I've been on many hikes around the area and most of them share common characteristics. There are trees, water, paths, and signs. Signs at the trailhead give an overview of the hike. Directional signs along the way indicate which path to take.

On that first hike to Roaring Run Falls, there were two signs more important than the directional ones—they were signs of warning. Amongst the beautiful scenery, there was danger lurking. The first sign was at the waterfall. As water poured over the rocks, directly in our path was a sign telling us to go no further. It warned to stay off the rocks and said "People have died." In the midst of the beauty was danger.

The second sign was on our way back to the car. Alongside the path was caution tape. Nothing looked particularly worrisome. There were some steps off the side of the path going into the woods but written on the tape were the words: "Copperheads nesting." "People have died."

Those were warnings we heeded. Yet without them, we could have easily entered into danger. I don't know where copperheads like to nest, and I wasn't looking for them. I was only looking at the beauty around us and enjoying the experience with no clue there was danger.

We needed these signs of warning on our hike, but we also need them in our lives. It's easy for us to look around and see beauty and goodness and be completely unaware that there is danger hiding. We need warning. When Jesus says, *"I am the door"* (John 10:9), he is telling us not only who he is, but he is also warning us about the dangers around us.

Jesus Warns

Our need for warning results from who we are. We are sheep. When we think of sheep, images of soft, cute, cuddly animals may come to mind, but we shouldn't think that about ourselves. In *A Shepherd Looks at Psalm 23*, Phillip Keller discusses various problems that sheep experience—they are uncreative when foraging for food, will follow trodden paths toward desolate places even though excellent food is nearby, are given to wandering, are timid and stubborn, are frightened at simple things, and are utterly defenseless. Sheep are directionless and weak. Left to themselves they will die because they are helpless.[1] This is the image that the Bible, and Jesus, presents of us. We are sheep.

The warning comes not only as a result of who we are but also because of the threat we encounter. Jesus speaks of *"thieves and robbers"* who come to the sheep to kill, steal, and destroy (John 10:10). From the context it appears that the "thieves and robbers" are the Pharisees. Preceding this discussion, Jesus had healed a man who was born blind. When questioned, the man told the Pharisees what Jesus had done. Instead of responding to this miracle with awe and celebration, the Pharisees called Jesus a *"sinner"* and said, *"We know that God has spoken to Moses, but as for this man* (Jesus)*, we do not know where he comes from"* (John 9:29). This is a clear attempt to discredit Jesus and turn the people away from him.

This threat that came upon Jesus' followers was spiritual in nature. The Pharisees were attempting to use their institutional authority as religious leaders to draw the healed man away from Christ. The threat worked on some. In John 10:22 we're told that the parents were afraid that the Pharisees would remove them from the synagogue. As a result of this fear, they would not speak in support of what Jesus had done.

Thus, the religious pressure of the Pharisees was leading people away from Jesus. What makes a threat like the Pharisees, or the tactics they employed, so dangerous is that they don't initially look too damaging. This is how threats often function, they don't look harmful. Yet, the things around us shape us, they inform how we live, and they reorder our desires. The danger is that we become so accustomed to the things around us, that we're unaware of how they're shaping us.

Think about it like this—I was born and raised in Canada. However, since the fall of 1997 I've lived in the United States and many of those years in South Carolina and Virginia. I've now lived here long enough that people no longer hear even the slightest Canadian accent. However, my wife will tell you that when I get around my Canadian family members or talk to them on the phone, a slight accent returns. I am completely unaware that it's happening. I don't hear the change in my voice, and I don't notice the return to a previous accent.

This example is clearly not morally problematic. However, the things that threaten us function similarly. We are surrounded by words, behaviors, and actions that shape our lives. We don't realize it's affecting us until it already has. Consider again the Pharisees. They were the religious leaders of the day. They knew the law better than anyone. From the outside they didn't look like a threat; they looked like they had the answers. But in reality, they were thieves and robbers because they opposed Jesus. This should cause us to examine our lives and ask "What are those things that look good, may in of themselves be good, but are threatening to displace Jesus? What are those things that we are putting our trust in and value more than Jesus?"

I had a man once tell me, "I wish my wife would look at me like I hung the moon." Is his desire for his wife to think well of him, to appreciate him, to love him, bad? Of course not. However, in the midst of desiring something beautiful, he wasn't able to see the danger of centering his life around his wife's approval. That is how threats work—they twist that which is good and put us in a place of danger. The Pharisees did this with their positions of authority and with God's law. Something good was being used to bring harm. Thus, Jesus warns us.

Jesus Calls

We also see that Jesus calls us. The image that Jesus puts before us is the entrance of a sheep pen. In verse 9 he says, *"I am the door. If anyone enters by me, he will be saved and will go in and out and find pasture."* The image of a pasture is used in Scripture to describe God's flourishing place and presence. In Psalm 23, David sings:

> *The Lord is my shepherd; I shall not want. He makes me lie down in green pastures. He leads me beside still water. He restores my soul. He leads me in paths of righteousness for his name's sake.* (Psa. 23:1–3)

There is a place for God's sheep to experience God's care. Sometimes in the Bible it's referred to as his kingdom. Here it's spoken of as the pasture. We enter this pasture of care through Jesus' calling. He says:

> *The sheep hear his voice, and he calls his own sheep by name and leads them out. When he has brought out all his own, he goes before them, and the sheep follow him, for they know his voice.* (John 10:3–4)

When Jesus calls his people, there is a sounding in our hearts of a faint echo of what we have always longed for but had never known until we heard it. It is the voice that reverberates throughout creation calling us to the one we've always needed. And we can't help but listen.

This is like an infant in the womb. Studies have shown that a baby can hear and make out its mother's voice even before it is born. Even before they can be held, they recognize the voice of their mother.[2] When Jesus calls, his sheep hear his voice. To his sheep, his call is one of a welcome into his presence.

Before we start getting full of ourselves for being called by Jesus or prideful that we are invited into his pasture, we need to remember why we're welcomed— only because Christ calls us. We are never told that we're called because of our virtue, talents, wealth, that we have the model family, or the best Sunday school attendance, etc. We are not welcomed or called because of anything in of ourselves. In Deuteronomy 7:6–8a God said to his people:

> *For you are a people holy to the LORD your God. The LORD your God has chosen you to be a people for his treasured possession, out of all the peoples who are on the face of the earth. It was not because you were more in number than any other people that the LORD set his love on you and chose you, for you were the fewest of all peoples, but it is because the LORD loves you....*

God called them to be his people because he loved them. The same is true for us. Jesus doesn't call us because we're the best of the best, or because we have much to offer, or because we're pious and needed just a little bit of direction—no! We're sheep! We were wandering around; we were aimless and lost. We, like Israel of old, were called by God only because of his love.

This reality should bring out a response of gratitude and humility. As those who have been called by Jesus, we should be the most thankful people in all the world. He has called us by name and led us into life. This is a life that we could not have acquired for ourselves. We have passed through a gate we could not have found by our own searching. Jesus had to call us for us to enter God's pasture.

Not only should we be the most thankful, but we should also be the humblest. I come from a theological tradition that values precision and theological accuracy. Precision and accuracy should be appreciated. However, theological correctness should cause us to be theologically correct about who we are: we're sheep! Undeserving of what God has done. Apart from him, lost forever. Humility should be one of the defining qualities of a Christian. As Richard Baxter wrote, "Humility is not a mere ornament of a Christian, but an essential part of the new creature. It is a contradiction in terms to be a Christian, and not be humble."[3] Theological precision should cause humility and gratitude to characterize those who have heard the call of our Lord.

Jesus Guards

Jesus' work on our behalf doesn't stop with calling us. He also guards us. In verses 7–8 Jesus says, *"Truly, truly, I say to you, 'I am the door of the sheep'... I am the door. If anyone enters by me, he will be saved and will go in and out and find pasture."* At first glance these words may not give the impression of guarding, but that has to do with our limited understanding of what a Middle Eastern sheep pen looked like.

There is a story told of Sir George Adam Smith. He was an Old Testament professor in Scotland during the late 1800s and early 1900s. On one occasion, he was travelling through the Middle East with a guide, and they came across a shepherd and his sheep. The shepherd took Smith to where he put his fold of sheep at night. The pen had four walls of rails with an entry way on one side. There was no swinging door or gate, simply an opening. The shepherd told Smith that at night, all his sheep went in, and they were perfectly safe because he was the door. That was the phrase the shepherd used. He wasn't a Christian, and he wasn't trying to invoke biblical imagery or language. But he said, "I am the door." The shepherd said, "When the light has gone, and all the sheep are inside, I lie in the open space, and no sheep ever goes out but across my body, and no wolf comes in unless he crosses my body; I am the door."[4]

The shepherd lays down in the opening and is the door that keeps the sheep safely inside. The shepherd is the gate that guards the sheep from threats. When Jesus said *"I am the door,"* he was not only saying that he is the entry point for which we have life but that he is also the guardian of that life. His sheep are perfectly safe. Those who have life *by* him, our life is maintained *through* him. He himself lays down and ensures that his sheep will never be lost.

Peter describes this reality when he writes that because of Jesus we have *"an inheritance that is imperishable, undefiled, and unfading, kept in heaven for you..."* (1

Peter 1:4). Peter is telling us that we are being guarded by God's power for the salvation to be revealed in the last day. The life we have in Christ has been given to us and nothing—not death or hell, not the devil or this world—can remove us from the care that we are given by Christ.

No enemy will get past him, and none of his sheep will be lost. Jesus lays himself down in the place of greatest danger. Thieves, robbers, and wolves would all seek access to the sheep but what they find is a door. A man who gave his life and rose again to guard his sheep.

4

THE GOOD SHEPHERD

John 10:11–21

I am the good shepherd. The good shepherd
lays down his life for the sheep.

We turn now to Jesus' fourth "I am" statement. In the previous chapter we saw how Jesus identified himself as the door. Yet in his discussion of who he is, he informs us of who we are—sheep. Continuing with that theme of sheep and the door to the pen, Jesus now calls himself "the Shepherd." One of the unique things about this particular identification compared to the other "I am" statements is that this is the only one that is personal. All the other statements are impersonal: door, way, vine, light, etc. But here he takes on for himself the personal title of "Shepherd."

Particular words can almost function like echoes of prior experiences that tell us something of what we should expect when you encounter them again. Smells, sounds, and words have become such a part of our experience that each time we come across certain ones, we associate them with an event or expectation. Pumpkin spice tells us it's fall, and "take me out to the ballgame" signals that it's time to stretch. As soon as we hear these sounds, smell these smells, or see these sights, we know what to expect.

I imagine the same is true when we hear the word "shepherd." As soon as you read that word, what came to your mind? If you've been around the church or read your Bible, there is a strong chance you thought of Psalm 23. As I mentioned previously, this is one of the most well-known psalms, and it begins, *"The Lord is my shepherd"* (Ps 23:1).

This is a good place to focus your thoughts. When we hear Jesus say he is the Good Shepherd, this should cause us to stop and recall what we know of the shepherd of the Old Testament. When we do this, we remember that God is our shepherd and our guide. Thus, we have this image of God, coupled with Jesus' self-identification of the same image, and it creates a connection that clearly indicates that Jesus was making a claim of divinity and of authority. This was not lost on his hearers.

To his hearers, Jesus' claims were so outrageous that they accused him of being demonic or crazy. John writes, *"There was again a division among the Jews because of these words. Many of them said, "He is a demon, and is insane; why listen to him?"* (John 10:19).

"Why listen to him?" That is a good question. Perhaps as you read this book and you hear the claims of Jesus, you are thinking "maybe the Jews were right, maybe these are the utterances of a crazy person." But before you disregard Jesus' statements, I want you to see why we should not only listen to him, but why we should follow him. We should follow him because as the Good Shepherd, Jesus pursues us.

He Pursues Us

In verse 16, Jesus says, *"And I have other sheep that are not of this fold. I must bring them also...."* He said, "I must." Not, I should; not, if I have time; I *must*. There is a sense of resolve and of urgency. Jesus must go into the fields, climb the mountains, and enter the cities to find his own. But who are these?

I already alluded to the language of shepherd and sheep harkening back to the Old Testament. Throughout the Old Testament, the Jewish people are described as God's sheep. One example of this is Psalm 100:3 *"Know that the LORD, he is God! It is he who made us, and we are his; we are his people, and the sheep of his pasture."*

But when Jesus speaks of his sheep, he doesn't limit

this to the Jewish people. He said, *"I have other sheep that are not of this fold..."* (John 10:16). By referring to these other sheep who are from another fold, Jesus is telling us that his sheep are not limited to an ethnic people, but it extends beyond that of Old Testament Israel. That's what he's saying in verse 16, *"And I have other sheep that are not of this fold. I must bring them also."* Jesus brings the nations into the people of God.

This gathering of sheep from other nations was the expectation of the Old Testament. From the first book of the Bible, Genesis, the promise that God makes is that he will shepherd the nations and call out his sheep from every tribe and tongue to follow him. This was made evident in Genesis 12. God said to Abraham, *"I will make you a great nation, and I will bless you and make your name great, so that you will be a blessing... and in you all the families of the earth shall be blessed"* (Gen.12:2–3).

The promise was that the nations would be blessed by God. That's what the Good Shepherd does—he brings blessing to the nations. He is going into the world, gathering his sheep, and bringing them into his fold. It was too small a thing for his heritage to be limited to only Israel. As Psalm 2 says, the nations will be his heritage, *"the ends of the earth your possession"* (Ps 2:8). There isn't a Jewish flock, a Gentile flock, and an American flock. There is one flock, made up of all the sheep that Jesus has pursued. Jesus doesn't only seek out his people. He also draws them into an intimate relationship.

He Draws Us In

In verse 14, Jesus says, *"I know my own and my own know me, just as the Father knows me and I know the Father."* Do you hear the intimacy with which Jesus knows us? *"As the Father knows me and I know the Father."* Jesus is making an incredible statement about our relationship with him. He likens his knowledge of us to that which he has of the Father. In one sense, this is astonishing. In another, it is unthinkable. The perfect knowledge by which the Father knows the Son and the Son knows the Father—it is that knowledge that Jesus has for us.

To be known with such intimacy could make us afraid. We don't want people to know us this deeply. In fact, we do a lot to ensure that we're not known. We function like the character Phil Woodward in the movie *The Company Men*, which takes place during the financial crisis of 2008–2009. Phil had worked his way up to be an executive. He has a nice house, drives a great car, his daughter got into a top-notch college, and to all his neighbors he looks great. But unknown to them is that he no longer has a job. He has been fired. His neighbors are unaware of this because every morning he gets up and puts on his suit, grabs his briefcase, and spends the day pretending he still has a job. He is hiding.

And so are we. We put on masks of false selves, minimize our actions so people won't prod, create virtual-identities that are facades, and confess only enough sin to stop people from asking. We are natural hiders, and we have been since Adam. That was Adam's first instinct after he sinned—to hide, and it has been our instinct since. We spend a great deal of time and energy trying to make sure no one will ever know what is in our minds and our hearts.

Thus, when we hear we are drawn into a relationship with Christ that has such intimacy, it may make us feel uncomfortable and afraid. It may cause us to want to try and hide from the Shepherd. But we can't hide from Jesus any more than Adam could hide from the Father. He knows us. All our thoughts, words, and deeds. He knows them all.

Before we allow fear and anxiety to overtake us, there is something about this knowledge that we cannot forget. Not only does Jesus know us, but the passage tells us we know him. What we know of him is that he is good. Others may know us and want nothing to do with us, but not Jesus. Others may know us and recoil, but Jesus comes near. He is good. He is trustworthy. He doesn't abuse his knowledge of us. His knowing us actually moves him to show how good he really is. We see his goodness by the fact that he defends us.

He Defends Us

When we think of a shepherd and sheep, perhaps the picture that comes to mind is the one that is often depicted in children's bibles. The shepherd has an angelic glow. He is kind and gentle, sitting in a fresh field of clover, the sun descending in the west, and sheep sitting quietly in his lap.

That may be a pretty picture, but it's not an accurate one. Yes, the shepherd intimately knows his sheep. He knows them by name. But the work of the shepherd is filled with danger and requires a great deal of strength and courage.

Before David was the king, he was a shepherd. Before David entered the field of battle to challenge the giant Goliath, he had to convince Saul to allow him to fight. Though David was confident and called the people to trust that he would be victorious, Saul had his doubts. He said to David, *"You are not able to go against this Philistine to fight with him, for you are but a youth, and he has been a man of war from his youth"* (1 Sam 17:33). In other words, "you're too small, too scrawny, too young, and too weak." David was not deterred, he responded, *"Your servant used to keep sheep for his father..."* (1 Sam 17:34a).

Now if we're operating out of the children's Bible shepherd point-of-view, David's words don't create confidence. If anything, if the weak shepherd is the picture in our minds, we would probably think that David is going to get slaughtered. However, he goes on to describe what a shepherd does:

> *Your servant used to keep sheep for his father. And when there came a lion, or a bear, and took a lamb from the flock, I*

went after him and struck him and delivered it out of his mouth. And if he arose against me, I caught him by his beard and struck him and killed him. (1 Sam. 17:34–35)

Shepherds weren't wimps. Shepherds were strong and courageous. They went to great lengths to defend their sheep.

That's what the Good Shepherd does. Look at how Christ contrasts himself with the hired hands. In verse 12, the wolf comes, and the hired hand flees to save himself. But not the shepherd! Four times (vv. 11, 15, 17, 18) in this passage Jesus says the Good Shepherd lays down his life for the sheep. He doesn't flee. He defends with his life. The Good Shepherd willingly sacrifices himself to the point of death in order to deliver his sheep.

Jesus continues to defend us even after his death. A human shepherd may give up his life for the sheep, but when he is gone, the sheep are left to fend for themselves. They continue to be in danger. Who will defend them when another wolf comes?

But that's not us. Yes, Jesus laid down his life for us. He sacrificed himself to deliver us, but he didn't leave us to fend for ourselves. Listen to what he says about his sacrifice: *"I lay it down on my own accord. I have authority to lay it down and I have authority to take it up again"* (John 10:18). Jesus is unique in his shepherding because he not only laid down his life by going to the cross, but he took it back up by rising again. In his death, when his blood was shed, our sin was atoned for. But it was in his resur-rection that death was defeated. The Good Shepherd rose to life to deliver us from eternal death. The tomb is empty. His death was unlike any other death because resurrection followed it.

Since Jesus knows us, defends us, and has made us part of his flock, we are his. As his flock, we are no longer our own, but we belong to him. This means that he leads us, and it also means that there is nothing that the Shepherd can't ask of us. There isn't a single aspect of our lives that doesn't belong to him.

As question one of the Heidelberg Catechism asks, "What is your only comfort in life and death?" It answers, "That I am not my own, but belong—body and soul, in life and in death—to my faithful Savior, Jesus Christ…."[1] For those who follow the Good Shepherd, we belong to him. Every part of us—our minds, abilities, possessions, families, time, vocations—they are all his.

If this were anyone else, it would cause us concern. If Jesus was a demon or a mad man, then we should be worried. But that's not who our Shepherd is. Jesus isn't merely a man. Jesus is God incarnate, the Good Shep-herd. By his death and resurrection, he not only claims us for himself, but he actually unites us to himself. We're not called to follow a mere man whose authority and ways will be detrimental to us, but we are called to follow the Good Shepherd who defends us and secures for us eternal life. Therefore, let us agree with those who said, *"These are not the words of one who is oppressed by a demon"* (John 10:21). And let us continue, "these are the words and actions of the Lord, the words and actions of the Good Shepherd."

5

LIFE WHEN EVERYTHING ISN'T AWESOME

John 11:17–27

*Jesus said to her, "I am the
resurrection and the life."*

E very one of us has experienced hurt or
disappointment, pain or discouragement. If you
haven't yet, you surely will. What do we do with that?
When a relationship fails, when expectations don't meet
reality, when a loved one dies—what do we do? It is into
this situation that Jesus enters; his friend has died, and in
the midst of the pain of death, he tells all who hear, *"I am
the resurrection"* (John 17:15). By doing this, Jesus is re-
orienting our response when sorrow comes into our
lives.

My family enjoys *The Lego Movie*. It's full of quirky characters, witty dialogue, and dry humor. Though there are many memorable lines, the thing that gets buried in your brain is a single phrase: "Everything is awesome!" These three words are the beginning of a song that functions as a theme to the movie. "Everything is awesome! Everything is cool when you're part of the team. Everything is awesome when we're living our dream."[1] The main character Emmitt embodies this posture towards the world. Every experience in his life is awesome—even the non-awesome things. For instance, he has no family, but that's not a problem because "everything is awesome." He pays $32 for a cup of coffee, it's okay because "everything is awesome." His friends and neighbors don't know his name and don't recognize him. No worries. Why? Because "everything is awesome." Everyone in the city of Bricksburg adopts this rose-colored view of the world. No matter your experience or your circumstance, everything is awesome.

For Emmitt, everything is awesome, and somewhere along the way, the church has adopted this mentality as well. We know that Jesus has saved us from eternal death, he has given us new life, we have purpose and identity, and so "everything is awesome." All those things are true: we do have new life, Christ has given us new purpose, and we have a new identity in him, but we live in a world where everything is not awesome.

What do we do when everything isn't awesome? Are we to simply spin pain and disappointment, to put on a smile that doesn't line up with an inward reality? Is this the Christian response? Think about the people in John 11: Mary, Martha, and their friends. Lazarus, their brother and friend has died. What is the proper Christian response to pain, hurt, and death? Since Jesus says, *"I am the resurrection and the life"* (John 11:25), does this mean that we are to gloss over the sadness we experience? Is Jesus' statement the biblical equivalent of *The Lego Movie's* theme song? Or does it mean something else?

What I want us to see is that while Jesus' claim of being the *"resurrection and the life"* is a triumphant statement of victory over death. It does not wash over our deepest experiences of pain. Instead, it allows us to be honest with the hurt and sorrow we feel. This passage helps us see how Jesus' claim of being the "resurrection" frees us to respond to death in a distinctly Christian way.

With Grief Instead of (False) Piety

This passage is filled with grief. We see it in Mary and Martha who are in need of consoling (v. 19) and among those who sought to comfort them (v. 33). The passage is filled with weeping and mourning. Yet even in the midst of this grief, Martha makes an incredible claim about who Jesus is and what he can do. She says, *"I know that whatever you ask from God, God will give you.... I know that he will rise again in the resurrection on the last day"* (John 11:22, 24). She's confident that her current experience isn't the end of the story.

This statement of hope could cause some to question if her tears and mourning are appropriate. No doubt, there may be well-intentioned people who would use the truth of who Jesus is and what he will do to encourage Martha to stop her weeping and to embrace this future hope in the midst of her present reality. If you've experienced loss, then you've heard this seemingly pious advice. Out of a desire to live with hope, people quickly move through grief and rush to praise.

My mother died of cancer in December 2003. Shortly after Christmas, my wife and I were at a conference for college students. During one of the times of worship, we were singing the praise song, "Blessed be your name."[2] Amongst the various stanzas, there is a bridge that says, "You give and take away, you give and take away, My heart will choose to say, Lord blessed be your name." There is no denying this is a biblical theme, these words are directly from Job 1:21. As we were singing this song, a friend came up to me and said, "Penny, even in your mom's death—blessed be the Lord." Before I say anything else, I want to be clear that I don't resent my friend for saying this. He was seeking to console and comfort me with God's truth. His statement was well intentioned. He was trying to help. His words had the sound of piety, but they gave little room for grief.

If this isn't the right way to approach those who are grieving, what is? Jesus shows us:

When Jesus saw her weeping, and the Jews who had come with her also weeping, he was deeply moved in his spirit and greatly troubled. And he said, 'where have you laid him?' They said to him, 'Lord, come and see.' Jesus wept." (John 11:33–35)

Though, *"Jesus wept"* is the shortest verse in the Bible, it is one of the most profound. The two words *"Jesus wept"* give us insight into how Jesus engaged with those who mourned. He didn't discount their suffering or minimize their sadness. He shared it. He wept. Jesus felt true sorrow for what had occurred to his friends.

If the one who is the resurrection and who triumphs over death, grieves over death, then we need to be free, and to free others, to grieve. When loss comes, be it through death or suffering, God invites us to grieve, and Jesus grieves with us.

Indignation Instead of Acceptance

Another way that we can try and respond to the pain of the world is to simply accept it. We've all heard that death is simply the natural progression of life. There is no question that death is a common experience in our world, one that we will all experience if the Lord does not return first. But acknowledging the reality of death isn't the same as being comfortable with it.

Jesus didn't accept death. He didn't shrug his shoulders and say, "That's just how things are." Instead, he showed indignation towards death. This is difficult to see at first glance, but the passage shows us Jesus' scorn for death. The words used in verse 33, *"deeply moved"* and *"greatly troubled,"* are rare and difficult to interpret.[3] To a casual reader, these words may suggest that Jesus was simply saddened at what had happened. However, these words "suggest anger, outrage or emotional indignation."[4] As one theologian said, "it is lexically inexcusable to reduce this emotional upset to the effects of empathy, grief, pain or the like."[5] Instead, Jesus was outraged at what had happened.

Jesus didn't accept death. He looked at it as his enemy. As Nicholas Wolterstorff wrote, "God is appalled by death."[6] He is displeased with death because death is an invader in God's good creation. Remember how God created the world—*"very good"* (Gen. 1:31). Before sin entered into the world, Adam and Eve were free from the pains and suffering that have become common in our world. They were created free from death. The natural way the world was formed was apart from this unnatural intruder. That's what death is—an unnatural intruder into God's natural world. We should be angry at death because death has scarred God's good creation.

If we accept death and suffering as just the way things are, then we are tacitly giving up a belief that things will get better. The philosopher Nietzsche understood this even though he was no friend of Christianity. He argued that those who do not believe in God should not listen to the cries of woe in the world but instead should ignore

the cries of sorrow and hurt and put aside a desire for a
better world.[7]

He was right.

If we do not believe in a good God, then we should
not long for goodness to come. If we accept death and
pain as our friend, we are giving up on the desire for
goodness and the belief that there is a kingdom to come.
Instead, Christians are to see those feelings of sadness
and anger, grief and mourning, as the result of a deep
knowledge that death is an invader that is not to be
embraced. Death is an unnatural inhabitant in God's
natural world. That is why Paul says in 1 Corinthians
15:26, *"The last enemy to be destroyed is death."* Jesus' identity as the *"resurrection and the life"* means that we are to
respond to pain, sorrow, and death with grief and indignation because things are not the way they are supposed
to be.

Hope Instead of Despair

If we were to leave it at that, then we would be in trouble
of falling into despair. However, Jesus' identity as the
resurrection gives us hope. In John 11, he tells his audi-
ence that the sadness they were experiencing isn't the
end of the story. We see this hope in Jesus' conversation
with Martha.

When Jesus first arrived, Martha expressed great faith
in who Jesus was and what he could do. We read:

> *Martha said to Jesus, 'Lord, if you had been here, my brother*
> *would not have died. But even now I know that whatever you*
> *ask from God, God will give you.' Jesus said to her, 'Your*
> *brother will rise again.' Martha said to him, 'I know that he*
> *will rise again in the resurrection on the last day.'"* (John
> 11:21–24)

Martha believed Jesus could have brought healing to her brother. She displayed faith that, though death was momentarily victorious, there is a resurrection to come. Her faith wasn't only about the future. She expressed a clear belief that Jesus could have done the miraculous in that moment. She said, *"Even now I know that whatever you ask..."* (John 11:22). You get the sense that she believed Jesus could accomplish anything, maybe even resurrection.

In his response to her, Jesus, affirmed her faith and gave her hope when he said, *"I am the resurrection and the life"* (John 11:25). The truth of resurrection isn't theoretical or far off. It isn't an abstract belief in a future day. It is personalized in the present. It is near. Jesus continued, *"Whoever believes in me, though he die, yet shall he live, and everyone who lives and believes in me shall never die, yet shall he live"* (John 11:25).

What Jesus is teaching us is that there are two aspects to this resurrection—there is a future aspect and an immediate one. For those who believe in him and die, we will live. With this in view, Jesus was affirming Martha's faith in the future resurrection. This future resurrection is alluded to in the Old Testament (cf. Dan. 12:2; Isa. 26:19; Ps. 49:15; 72:20; etc.) and affirmed in the New Testament (cf. John 5:29; Acts 4:33; 24:25; 1 Cor. 6:14; 15:1–58; etc.).

Along with this future aspect, there is also an immediate aspect to resurrection. When Jesus says, *"everyone who lives and believes in me shall never die"* (John 11:26), he's speaking of the final resurrection that has already begun. The way the Bible talks about the relationship of believers to Jesus is that what has occurred to him is now credited to us. In Romans 6 and Colossians 3, Paul declares that believers in Jesus have been raised with Christ. This is already part of our existence. We have been united to Christ in his death and also in his resurrection. This means that the future resurrection we wait for has already been credited to us now.

The fact that we are united to Jesus in his resurrection has significant implications for our life. It means that we are to live in our present moment as people of hope.

Hope is not wish fulfillment or naïve optimism. Biblical hope is rooted in the resurrection. The reason why we can grieve and have righteous anger while not falling into despair is because we are upheld by resurrection hope.

This is a hope that is built out of reality. Jesus didn't simply claim to be the resurrection and the life, he showed it. He approached the tomb, he told them to roll away the stone, and he cried out, *"Lazarus, come out"*

(John 11:43). And Lazarus did. Jesus' voice pierced through the silence of death and awakened Lazarus to new life. Jesus was showing us that he has the final word over death and because of that we have hope.

This hope was on display for my wife and I when her granddad passed away. Kat's Nana and granddad had been married for sixty-two years. They lived through a war, raised two children, and helped to raise two grandchildren. They would sit together at the kitchen table and pay their bills. Granddad would ride with Nana to the grocery store simply to be with her, and she knew exactly how he liked his sandwich. Sixty-two years they lived together, and at the end, Nana was with him. At his bedside, holding his hand, knowing he was nearing death, sad that her husband was about to leave her, Nana looked at her daughter and said, "Tell him he can go, Cheryl. Tell him he can go."

In the midst of the sorrow of losing her husband and knowing the grief that would come, how could she say, "Tell him he can go"? She had a hope stronger than grief and more powerful than indignation. She knew the resurrection was true. There was a biblical, past resurrection that we are united to and a resurrection still yet to come.

6

PEACE FROM THE TRUTH

John 14:1–7

Jesus said to him, "I am the way,
and the truth, and the life. No one
comes to the Father except through me."

As we've been looking at these different "I am"
statements, I hope it's evident that these aren't
theoretical propositions. Jesus' various descriptions
come about in particular situations. The statements are
not ahistorical but are spoken into a circumstance to
bring comfort, lead the disciples from trouble, or elicit a
hopeful faithfulness amongst those who hear.

John 14 is no different. Jesus speaks to his disciples in

a time when they were filled with anxiety, and his words give them peace.

When we leave something familiar or someone leaves us—whether it is moving to a new city, your kid's first night at summer camp, or going off to college—we feel unsure and anxious. When my wife and I left Greenville, South Carolina to move to St. Louis to attend seminary, I experienced these emotions. There we were with all our worldly possessions in a moving truck. We had a two-week-old baby, and we left behind a job, a church, and friends. We were moving to a city where I had no job, we didn't know anyone, and didn't know where we would go to church. Everything was unknown. Would we find community? Would we have friends? Was this a huge mistake? What if I was wrong in thinking this was how the Lord was leading? Sadness, fear, and worry filled my mind and heart.

The disciples were experiencing a similar emotion in this passage. At the end of chapter 13, Jesus told the disciples that he was leaving them. There is no doubt the disciples were immediately overcome with worry.

You can hear the concern building in the passage. Jesus says in verse 4, *"You know the way to where I am going."* Then Thomas replied anxiously, *"Lord, we do not know where you are going. How can we know the way?"* (John 14:5). Jesus had been with them. He had been leading and directing them, and now he was about to leave them. They would be alone. They were unsure of the way forward.

Like the disciples, we too know the anxiety that comes with not knowing what will come. Our lives can at times feel like we are driving through unfamiliar country without a map, signs, or any direction of where we are going. We all experience these moments of relational, vocational, and familial anxiety, so we find ourselves sounding like Thomas, "Lord, where are you? Where are you leading? I don't know the way."

It's in response to this anxiety laden situation, Jesus says, *"Let not your hearts be troubled. Believe in God; believe also in me"* (John 14:1). Believing in Jesus is trusting him when he says, *"I am the way, the truth, and the life"* (John 14:6). Jesus counteracts our anxiety with a peace that comes from him being *"the way, the truth, and the life."* Jesus' identity is a source of comfort for the anxious heart because Jesus' statement reveals a particular path for his people.

A Particular Path

Jesus leads his people on an exclusive path. This is the primary way many of us think about this passage. When we discuss the exclusivity of Jesus—the claim that the uniqueness of Christianity is not simply a conception formed by Christians but is actually founded upon Christ's teaching—this is often the passage we'll turn to. Jesus not only said that he is *"the way, the truth, and the life,"* but he goes on to say, *"No one comes to the Father except through me"* (John 14:6). Not "some can." Not, "there is a loophole." "No one" comes to the Father except through Christ.

This type of a claim isn't well received in our culture. The exclusivity of Jesus is problematic for many. We are told that anyone who would hold such a position is intolerant and arrogant. Thus, when faced with this sort of challenge, it would be easy for the church to acquiesce and bend.

But this is one of the foundational teachings of the Christian faith. There is only *"one Lord, one faith, one baptism"* (Eph. 4:5), one way to God: Jesus.

This challenges many of the notions our culture has about Jesus. Some want to reduce him to one religious option among many, a great moral teacher, a wise sage, or a pious man whose life should be emulated. While he was moral, wise, and led an exemplary life, Jesus is far more than that. He declared himself to be *the* Savior. Therefore, the only real options before us are to see him as a liar who pulled off the greatest hoax the world has ever seen or to see him as the Lord of the universe.[1] To our modern ears, this may still sound narrow-minded or arrogant.

But I want you to notice that Jesus didn't speak these words out of arrogance. He said them out of love for his disciples and for us. This is a love that wanted to lead us from divergent paths that would end in destruction. Jesus' path is not just exclusive, it's also directional.

The implication of an exclusive path that leads to life is that all other paths are destructive. There are many things we experience that are pulling not just for our attention and our affections but for our very lives. Often these look very appealing, but by giving our lives to these things that promise fulfillment, they will ultimately leave us empty. They are false paths instead of being the true one.

This isn't simply a Christian articulation of the world. Even non-Christians understand the fruitlessness of seeking life in things of the world. The writer David Foster Wallace argued that the path of money, possessions, beauty, sexual allure, power—these things that he claimed we worship and give ourselves to—they will eat us alive.[2] Wallace understood that these were not the paths that lead to life.

When Jesus said he is *"the way, the truth, and the life,"* he was directing us away from those things that devour and directing us to himself. In verse 3, he said that he goes before us *"to prepare a place for you... and will take you to myself, that where I am you may also be."* In other words, Jesus leads us to himself, not just for the immediate but also for the day to come. He directs us away from what would destroy and leads us to himself, the one who gives life.

Jesus' path leads us to life, and that means it is all-encompassing because it involves the entirety of our lives. The fact that Jesus claims there is only one way, one truth, and one life, means that every aspect of our lives is to be oriented towards that truth, that way, and that life. Therefore, we can't say with consistency that Jesus is the way, but I can find my own way to God. Or that he is the truth but what I believe to be true is derived from something else. If he is the truth and the way and the life, then he demands every part of our lives to be given over to him. As Holly Ordoway notes, the implication of assenting to the truths of Christianity requires a "radical commitment...that...was nothing whatsoever like the 'accept Jesus and be sure you'll get into heaven' idea...."[3] Jesus demands every part of us: our minds, our hearts, our desires, and all our actions are his to be directed.

This is why in verse 12 he says, *"Truly, truly, I say to you, whoever believes in me will also do the works that I do...."* Jesus' expectation is that our lives will be lived in a way that reflects his truth. The implication of this is that it's not just all-encompassing for our private lives, but it's all-encompassing for our public lives. We measure everything we experience against him. We don't accept what the world says to be true or the cultural commitments of the day blindly, we weigh them against the truth of the Gospel. We can affirm what is true in the world – even when it's spoken by those who are not Christians. But it also means that we challenge that which is not true. That is the posture we're often going to have – that of affirmation and challenge. This is why I can quote positively a writer like David Foster Wallace while at the same time opposing his perspective about God. In order to live out this affirmation-challenge posture, we'll need wisdom to sort through the various ideas of our world and our own hearts. We live in complicated times which are made

even more complicated by the fact that we're complicated beings. However, Jesus doesn't leave us to our
worries, he guides us. He is the personal truth by which
we measure everything by.

Therefore, as we follow along this particular path, we
are following a particular person.

A Particular Person

Our world values efficiency. There are times when
personal connection can be considered inefficient, and
they are laid aside. Think about the primary ways we
communicate—text, email, and private messages. These
are efficient but not often personal. These methods of
communicating are not bad in and of themselves. They
can be quite helpful. If I'm running late, I can send a text
to let my appointment know. If I'm trying to set up a
lunch, an email is easy. Our person-less efficiencies can
be helpful, but we often need something more.

There was a season in the life of my family when we
would eat at Red Robin for birthdays. A few years ago,
we noticed a change in their procedures. They had
adopted what was the equivalent of an electronic waiter.
A tablet sat on the table. We were to use it to order our
food, request another drink, play games, and pay our bill
without having to engage with an actual waiter or wait-
ress. This can be very helpful when the meal is over and
you're ready to leave. You don't have to wait for the
server to get your card and bring you your receipt.

It's great. Until it doesn't work. The first time using this "efficient" method, I swiped my card to pay, I noticed we were not given our free birthday burger. No matter how many times or different ways I tried, it wouldn't work. In the midst of my growing frustration, annoyance, and impatience, I needed a person, the server or manager, to solve our problem.

I needed a person. That's what Jesus gives us—a person. In fact, he gives himself. It's easy to reduce Jesus' statements and teachings to mere theological doctrines and truisms, but doctrine alone doesn't give us comfort, and truths by themselves do not provide peace. After all, James wrote that even the demons believe the truths of God (James 2:19), but their acknowledgement is not enough to bring them peace. They shudder at the truth. Thus, we can't miss that when Jesus says, *"I am the way and the truth and the life,"* that he is pointing us to a person.

Jesus doesn't say, "I know the way, I know the truth, I know the life." He says, *"I am."* What is true, what is right, and what is life—these are not philosophical categories or moralistic ideals that we give assent to, they are personified in Jesus. Truth apart from divine truth and a relationship with Christ is what Chesterton called the "suicide of thought."[4] There is no life apart from relationship with Jesus. The peace we are searching for is encompassed in a personal, following, loving relationship with Christ.

This relationship isn't just with him but also with the

Father. Jesus said that he leads us to the Father (v. 6), that knowing Jesus means we know the Father (v. 7), and that he goes to prepare a place for us in his Father's house (v. 2). Those who have a relationship with Jesus will dwell with him in the house of his Father. That's what is described in verse 3: *"I will come again and will take you to myself, that where I am you may also be."* Jesus has gone away, but he will return. When that happens, he doesn't simply give us conformation that our theological understandings have been true; he gives us himself and leads us to the Father. He gives us a person. A person that leads to peace.

7

ABIDING IN THE VINE

John 15:1–11

I am the true vine, and
my Father is the vinedresser.

W e've come to the last of Jesus' "I am" statements, and this one takes place in the midst of Jesus' farewell discourse. Jesus was preparing to depart this world and ascend into heaven. Though he was about to leave soon, Jesus gave his disciples an instruction. They were to remain in him, to abide in the vine.

In 2014, there was a song that was on the lips of many young girls. It was the title track from the movie *Frozen*. "Let It Go" won a Grammy and an Oscar. This catchy song became the theme of Queen Elsa's life. She had the magical power of controlling ice and snow, but she had trouble controlling it, and as a result, she was encouraged to hide it. After years of living alone in obscurity, she announced she was going to "let it go."

Let it go, let it go
Turn away and slam the door
It's time to see what I can do
To test the limits and break through
No right, no wrong, no rules for me
I'm free! Let it go, let it go
Here I stand, And here I'll stay[1]

She will no longer be hidden away or be bound by others: "No right, no wrong, no rules for me, I'm free!"

The song is picking up the same theme as the poem *Invictus* by William Ernst Henley. He wrote: "I am the master of my fate: I am the Captain of my soul."[2] This is the theme of self-actualization, the idea that an individual is the ultimate determining factor of one's life. Autonomy and self-actualization are consistent messages communicated through both high culture and pop culture. This belief in autonomy permeates nearly every part of our existence.

Before we adopt this posture as right, we should ask how it's going. If we're honest—it's not going well because of how easily we are swayed and moved by opinion. If we are really these self-authenticating, autonomous people, then why does someone else's opinion of us matter so much? Why does someone's online personality make us jealous? Why does someone's success fill us with resentment? Why does someone's failure make us feel superior?

Perhaps these are hints that we're not as autonomous as we like to think. We were never intended to be autonomous creatures. We are designed to be dependent on a life-giving source that is outside us. That's what Jesus tells us in this passage. When he says, *"I am the vine; you are the branches"* (John 15:5), he's telling us that we're not autonomous, but we're to be dependent on him because he is the source of life.

The Source of Life

The analogy that Jesus employed is clear. Shoots and branches only have life when they are connected to the vine. If they are broken off or removed, the branches will die. Thus, apart from Jesus who is the vine, we don't have life.

If you've been around the church for any length of time, this idea isn't new. I imagine that many who read this book will readily affirm that Jesus is the source of life. Yet even as we agree with this, we should see something that is easily missed. Jesus doesn't simply say he is the vine. He says, *"I am the true vine"* (John 15:1) Why does he include this adjective, "true"?

The language of "vine" is an Old Testament theme. A number of times throughout the Old Testament, Israel was called the vine. In Psalm 80:8, the psalmist writes, *"You brought a vine out of Egypt; you drove out the nations and planted it."* This is clearly a reference to Israel.

The psalmist goes on: *"You cleared the ground for it; it took deep root and filled the land. The mountains were covered with its shade, the mighty cedars with its branches. It sent out its branches to the sea and its shoots to the River"* (Ps. 80:9–11). The psalmist was declaring that God's people as the vine were to extend blessing to the nations. They were to cover the mountains with shade and send out their branches to the sea. They were to fill the earth. This was a mission Israel sadly failed to fulfil. The prophets Isaiah, Jeremiah, and Hosea all refer to Israel as this vine, but they each note the vine's failure to produce fruit (cf. Isa. 5; Jer. 2:21, Hosea 10:1–2).

Thus, when Jesus said he was the *true vine*, he was making a statement of contrast. Jesus was declaring he was the true and better Israel. Where Israel failed, he succeeded. But not just Israel. Where everything else fails, Jesus succeeds. I already mentioned how we search for ways to find life. Those efforts are like Kudzu, a vine that destroys life. Jesus, however, is the true vine that brings life. This life that he gives, he gives out of love.

Life Given Out of Love

Jesus displays his love by uniting us to himself. In verse 9, he says to those who abide in him, *"As the Father has loved me, so have I loved you."* This verse is important for our understanding of our relationship with the True Vine. It would be easy for many of us to focus our attention on verse 10: *"If you keep my commandments, you will abide in my love...."* We do need to give attention to this, but before we run to keeping Christ's commands, we need to hear why we keep them. Verse 9 tells us why, *"I loved you."* Before we are told to obey, follow, and keep, he says "I have first loved you." We abide in Christ because Christ has loved us and united us to himself.

Christ's love is not only reflected in the fact that we are united to the vine, but love is shown to us while we abide in Christ. This is reflected by the fact that the Father removes unproductive growth. His pruning demonstrates his love for us. That's what we see in verses 1–2:

> I am the true vine, and my Father is the vine dresser. Every branch in me that does not bear fruit he takes away, and every branch that does bear fruit he prunes.

If plants are left unattended, they will develop unproductive growth. In tomato plants, suckers will grow at the elbow where a shoot comes off of the stem. A gardener can leave those suckers to continue to grow. However, if she prunes them, energy in the plant is given to producing fruitful growth. By pruning the unwanted growth, the plant can produce more abundantly. The same is true of us. The Father, who is the *"vinedresser"* (John 15:1), prunes us. But that begs the question, "What

does this pruning entail?" This is a metaphor that refers
to our spiritual lives; it is a pruning of sin. This idea is
similar to that of Hebrews 12:7–11 where we are told
that God disciplines his children for their good.

Our first instinct isn't to think of God's pruning
discipline as good. It's normal to recoil at the idea since
discipline often hurts. However, the removal of our sin,
regardless of the pain that may come with it, is needed
for us to grow to maturity. And it is not something we
can do ourselves.

If you're a Christian reading this, then you probably
have no problem speaking of your sin. We acknowledge
it in our conversations, we confess it in our worship
services, and we give a nod to it when it's spoken of
generally. Yet, for all our acknowledgment of our sin, we
are often blind to it. Because of this, we need others who
are willing to lovingly show us our sin.

But who wants their sin exposed? It is often painful,
but it is needed.

I can clearly remember the times when a friend has
pointed out my critical spirit, biting tongue, or insensi-
tive joke. In those moments when they called me on my
sin, I wanted to protect myself from the pain by giving an
excuse, getting defensive, or dismissing it outright.
However, as the Spirit worked in my heart, I came to see
that having my sin revealed was for my good. God used
these people to reveal things about myself that I was
blind to. God used these friends to do what I could not
do on my own, to see my sin with clarity and prune my

sin. Though it may be painful, God's pruning of us is for our good. This is God's care and love to us. It's a love that prunes and produces.

Love That Produces Fruit

This is what abiding in the vine does—it produces fruit. Jesus said, *"By this my Father is glorified, that you bear much fruit and so prove to be my disciples"* (John 15:8). Ultimately the fruit that is produced in our lives is that of Christlikeness. This is the implication of abiding in the vine.

The branch of a grape vine produces grapes. Not oranges. Not apples. Grapes. If a branch that is connected to a grape vine produced tomatoes, we would think there is something wrong with that plant. Thus, when we apply the analogy to our union with Christ, the conclusion is clear—the fruit we are to produce must be in keeping with the vine we are connected to. Jesus said, *"If you keep my commandments, you will abide in my love, just as I have kept my Father's commandments and abide in his love"* (John 15:10). Christ has been obedient to the Father, so we are to obey Christ, and in doing so we are manifesting fruit.

For most of us, the idea of bearing fruit as a result of being connected to Christ makes sense. However, we might have questions about that little word in verse 5, *"much."* How much is much? Who decides what much is? That word can cause us to compare, to compete with others, or to think too little or too highly of ourselves.

But your fruitfulness is not determined by the perceived maturity of another, and "much" isn't defined as your advancement beyond another. Jesus said in the parable of the four soils that some will bear fruit *"a hundredfold, some sixty, some thirty"* (Matt. 13:8, 23). In other words, we don't know what "much" is for one another. We know that our own "much" is determined only by Christ. This should free us from comparing our maturity to others. We can focus our attention on abiding in the vine.

Finally, this fruit reveals that we do in fact belong to Christ. That's what the end of verse 8 tells us when Jesus says, *"you bear much fruit and so prove to be my disciples."* As we are connected to the vine and are bearing fruit, as we look more and more like Christ. We show that we are his people. It is our fruit that reflects we are united to him.

8

CONCLUSION: I AM NOT

John 1:19–28

He confessed, and did not deny,
but confessed, "I am not the Christ."

T he French theologian John Calvin said, "True and
sound wisdom consists in two parts: the knowledge of God and of ourselves."[1] Following Calvin, let's
make sure we look at both God and ourselves. For the
last seven chapters we've focused on our knowledge of
Jesus. Before we finish, I want to take a look at one more
statement from the gospel of John. This one isn't spoken
by Jesus, and it informs us about who we are. More
specifically—it helps us know who we are not.

A "humblebrag" has become part of our cultural

vernacular. It is defined as "making a modest or self-deprecating statement with the actual intent of drawing attention to something of which one is proud."[2] A humblebrag looks like tweeting "Oh man, it was a rough morning. I only ran fifteen miles." Or "too bad my kid has to settle for her second choice of schools—Harvard." The humblebrag is a way for us to glory in ourselves without sounding glorious, being proud while sounding humble.

We employ this way of making ourselves glorious because we know that arrogance and pride are not culturally prized. No one likes the guy who is always bringing attention to himself, and we roll our eyes at overtly proud people. But deep in our hearts, we want to be acknowledged, honored, and we want glory.

Jesus calls us to resist the very thing we want. I hope that as we've considered Jesus' "I am" statements, we've seen that the one who is deserving of our boasting isn't the person we see in the mirror. It's the person these seven statements are about.

John the Baptist understood this. He had the opportunity to take glory for himself, but instead, he resisted glory.

Resisting Glory

In order to resist the glory Jesus deserves, we need to know ourselves. In this passage, there are a couple of ways John shows he had an accurate understanding of who he was. The first is the most obvious. When the priests and the Levites came to inquire about him, we're told, *"He confessed, and did not deny, but confessed, 'I am not the Christ'"* (John 1:20). John identified himself not with who he was, but who he was not. This is counter to how we often present ourselves. When was the last time you introduced yourself to someone with who you are not? When asked about your profession, would you say three things you don't do? This isn't our normal behavior. We present the positive qualities about ourselves, but that's not what John did. This wasn't for a lack of admirable qualities.

From the little we know of John, he had an impressive life and unique experiences. Consider some of what John could have told them: his birth was foretold by an angelic messenger (Luke 1:13–17). His parents were beyond the age when they could have children. Thus, his birth was miraculous (Luke 1:18). In his mother's womb he was filled with the Spirit (Luke 1:15). He could have talked for hours about who he was and how God had set him apart, but he didn't lead with any of these impressive qualities. John didn't claim his own glory. Instead he declared, *"I am not."*

John rightly confessed that he was not the Christ, but he said more than that. When he spoke of Jesus, he said that the Christ to come is so great, that John wasn't worthy to tie his sandals (John 1:27). In the culture where John was living, a student would serve his master in every way except for removing his sandals. That was the work of a slave.[3] Therefore, John was telling his listeners that in comparison to the Christ, he was less than even a slave. He was not even worthy to do the tasks that a slave was required to do.

If we could interject our modern-day assessments onto John's statement, what would people say? Perhaps we'd hear things like, "John, that's not true. You're great." "Don't be too hard on yourself." Or "What you need is more self-esteem." However, John wasn't being self-despising or self-deprecating. He was resisting self-glorification and embracing true humility. "I am not worthy. I am not the Christ."

You know who else needs to say this? We do.

I had a seminary professor who would have his students say various statements at the beginning of each class. Statements like "Good morning Jay (his name was Jay)" and "Start with the bible not with a commentary." Along the way, he added an additional statement to the students' recitation: "I am not the Christ."

This is an important statement for future pastors to make. It is easy for pastors and leaders to believe and function as though they are the solution to the church's problems. Yet, I am not the Christ.

This isn't just a reality for those in church leadership. Parents, teachers, counselors, friends, children—regardless of who we are or the position we have, it is easy for us to act as though what the people around us need is us. We swoop in and take control of a situation. We make all our children's decisions. We share our opinions about "best" practices, so people can be more like we are. We would never verbally say, "I am the Christ," but our actions often betray that we want to be the hero of all the stories.

That is not your responsibility. It is not your calling. You are not the Christ.

Knowing Our Role

If we're going to resist taking the glory that we are not afforded, we need to know not only ourselves but also our roles. John's role was an interesting one. He was given the job of being a herald, a voice crying out to give attention to another. He said, *"I am the voice of one crying out in the wilderness, 'Make straight the way of the Lord'"* (John 1:23). This may seem minor to us, but it was a significant job. John was fulfilling the prophecy spoken by Isaiah in Isaiah 40:3. Thus, John's role was important, but it was still a subservient role. He was a voice declaring that someone better is coming.

I imagine that many who are reading this haven't heard of Paul D. Irving. While you may not know his name, there is a good chance you've seen him. In January 2012, Irving became the House of Representatives Sergeant at Arms. He has a variety of responsibilities which includes announcing the President at the State of the Union address. You've seen him on television. Before the President enters the House, the Sergeant at Arms cries out, "Mr. Speaker! The President of the United

States!" And then he stands aside, making way for the President to walk in. In that moment, his job is to announce and proclaim that another has come. He gathers everyone's attention to redirect their focus on someone else. That's what John was doing. He pointed to Christ. He wasn't supposed to glorify himself. He focused attention on Jesus Christ.

That wasn't just John's responsibility. It's ours too. John's role was unique in that he was the one the Old Testament spoke of as making way for the Lord. But every follower of Jesus should point others to Christ. We don't make the way of the coming of the Lord, for he has already come. However, we do declare to the world that the Christ has come. The Apostle Paul said, *"For what we proclaim is not ourselves, but Jesus Christ as Lord"* (2 Cor. 4:5). We resist taking glory for ourselves by making much of Jesus, pointing others to him, and giving him the glory he deserves.

Giving Glory

We give Jesus glory because of who he is and what he has done. John said, *"Make straight the way of the Lord"* (John 1:23). John tells us that Jesus is—the Lord. As I already mentioned, John is speaking of a prophecy by Isaiah. The hope of the entire Old Testament was centered on the coming of the Messiah, the Christ, who is the Lord. His coming was not only the hope of the Old Testament. It's the hope of the nations. Ever since sin entered the world in Genesis 3, the world has been looking for and hoping for someone to deal with the problem of sin. When John said the Lord is coming, he was declaring that the King they had been waiting for had arrived. His arrival means that he will deal with the rebellion of this world. He will accomplish what only the Christ could accomplish. He would redeem his people, not by arms or ammunition. The Lord brings redemption by being the Lamb.

After this passage, on the following day, Jesus came towards John. When John saw Jesus, he said, *"Behold, the Lamb of God, who takes away the sin of the world"* (John 1:29). Jesus is not only the Lord who comes to rule over us. He's the lamb of God who lays down his life. In sacrificial contexts, the purpose of the lamb is to be slaughtered, for blood to be shed, for atonement to be made. That's Jesus, the lamb of God who has come to *"take away the sins of the world."* Jesus is the greater lamb; he is the greatest lamb. His single sacrifice would atone for all the sins of all his people. This is who he is. This is why he came.

When we understand who Jesus is and what he came to accomplish, it causes us to give him glory.

Think about it like this—you're in Washington DC, going from monument, to museum, to memorial, and you come to the World War II Memorial. You walk around the plaza and read about the heroic acts the soldiers performed.

As you take it all in and consider what they accomplished, you know what you don't think about? All the things you've done. You don't walk up to the stranger across the way and start reminiscing about your high school football successes or the promotion you were awarded or the number of degrees you've earned. As you look at that memorial, you don't think about yourself at all. We're in awe of what *they* did, we celebrate *their* accomplishment, and we honor *their* sacrifice.

It should be even more so when we are confronted by Christ's care, accomplishment, and sacrifice. When we consider Jesus, we can't help but be humbled and give him honor.

John quotes Isaiah 40 which gives us the picture of a royal procession:

"Make straight in the desert a highway for our God. Every valley shall be lifted up, and every mountain and hill be made low; the uneven ground shall become level, and the rough places a plain. And the glory of the Lord shall be revealed, and all flesh shall see it together for the mouth of the Lord has spoken." (Is. 40:3–5).

A road that is straight, level, and free from obstacles. A path for the Lord to walk so all would see him and give him the glory that he deserves because he is the Lord over our lives, and he is the lamb who laid down his life.

As I've read this passage and thought more about John the Baptist, I am amazed by what he did and spoke. After all, he was a man worthy of honor. He was upright, pious, and humble. If there was a man who could be worthy of glory, surely, he would be at the top of the list. Yet he resists glorifying himself, and instead gives glory to Christ. He didn't seek to take glory for himself, and yet Jesus gave him honor. Jesus said of John, *"Truly, I say to you, among those born of women there has arisen no one greater than John the Baptist"* (Matt. 11:11a). What beautiful words! Not simply because they honor John, but because of who said them. Jesus honored John, but not only John.

Jesus gives honor to others as well. For he continued and said, *"Yet the one who is least in the kingdom of heaven is greater than he"* (Matt. 11:11b). Jesus tells us that those who do not seek their own glory will find it. The humble will be exalted, and the lowly will be lifted up because the Lord, the Lamb of God, will honor his disciples. He'll be standing before his Father in heaven and acknowledging us as his own. Therefore, let us not seek to take hold of a glory that is not ours. Instead, let us give glory to the one who is the Lord and the Lamb. Let us give glory to the one who is the Christ. Let us embrace with our hearts and say with our lips, "I am not the Christ."

NOTES

Who Do You Say He Is?

1. Leon Morris, *The Gospel According to John,* revised ed., The New International Commentary on the New Testament (Grand Rapids, MI: Wm B. Eerdmans Publishing Co., 1995), 323.
2. Ibid, 420.

1. Bread for the Hungry

1. By saying this, I don't intend to downplay the importance of day-to-day, moment-by-moment obedience. Jesus is concerned with our following him in the midst of the mundane, but in this passage, his emphasis is on the eternal.
2. Augustine, *Homilies on 1 John 4.6,* in *Augustine: Later Works,* ed. John Burnaby (Philadelphia: Westminster, 1955), 290, quoted in James K.A. Smith, *Desiring the Kingdom: Worship, Worldview, and Cultural Formation* (Grand Rapids, MI: Baker Academic, 2009), 50-1 n 20.

3. The Door

1. Philip Keller, *A Shepherd Looks at Psalm 23* (Grand Rapids, MI: Zondervan, 1977), 61, quoted in R. Kent Hughes, *John: That You May Believe,* Preaching the Word Series, ESV ed. (Wheaton, IL: Crossway, 2014), 267.
2. Lee Dye, "Babies Recognize Mom's voice from the Womb," ABC News, January 7, 2006, accessed November 16, 2020, https://abc-news.go.com/Technology/story?id=97635&page=1.
3. Richard Baxter, *The Reformed Pastor,* abridged by Daniel Wilson (Glasgow: William Whyte & Co., 1829), 86 quoted in Christopher

A. Hutchinson, *Rediscovering Humility: Why the Way Up is Down* (Greensboro, NC: New Growth Press, 2018), 34.

4. G. Campbell Morgan, *The Gospel According to John* (Westwood, NJ: Revell, n.d.), 177 quoted in Hughes, *John,* 271.

4. The Good Shepherd

1. Zacharias Ursinus, "The Heidelberg Catechism," A Puritan's Mind, accessed November 16, 2020, https://www.apuritansmind.com/creeds-and-confessions/the-heidelberg-catechism-by-zacharias-ursinus/.

5. Life When Everything Isn't Awesome

1. *The Lego Movie,* directed by Christopher Miller and Phil Lord (Warner Bros., 2014).
2. Matt Redman, "Blessed Be Your Name," by Matt Redman and Beth Redman, recorded 2002, ThankYou Music.
3. Colin G. Kruse, *John: An Introduction and Commentary*, Tyndale New Testament Commentaries, vol. 4, ed. Leon Morris (Downer's Grove, IL: Intervarsity Press, 2003), 249.
4. D.A. Carson, *The Gospel According to John*, The Pillar New Testament Commentary, (Grand Rapids, MI: Wm. B. Eerdmans Publishing Co., 1991), 415.
5. Ibid.
6. Nicholas Wolterstorff, *Lament For A Son* (Grand Rapids, MI: Wm. B. Eerdmans Publishing Co., 1987), 66.
7. Timothy Keller, *The Reason for God: Believe in an Age of Skepticism* (New York: Dutton, 2008), 152.

6. Peace From The Truth

1. C.S. Lewis expands on this in greater detail in, C.S Lewis, *Mere Christianity*, HarperCollins edition (San Francisco: HarperCollins Publishers, Inc., 2001), 52.

2. David Foster Wallace, *This is Water* (New York: Little, Brown and Company, 2009), 102–106.
3. Holly Ordoway, *Not God's Type: An Atheist Academic Lays Down Her Arms* (Chicago: Moody Publishers, 2010), 126–27.
4. G.K. Chesterton, "The Suicide of Thought," in *Heretics / Orthodoxy*, (Nashville, TN: Thomas Nelson, Inc., 2000), 191–204.

7. Abiding in The Vine

1. *Frozen*, directed by Chris Buck and Jennifer Lee (Walt Disney Animation Studios, 2013).
2. William Ernest Henley, "Invictus," Poetry Foundation, accessed November 16, 2020, https://www.poetryfoundation.org/poems/51642/invictus.

8. Conclusion: I Am Not

1. John Calvin, *The Institutes of the Christian Religion*, vol. 1, ed. John T. McNeill, trans. Ford Lewis Battles (Louisville, KY: Westminster John Knox Press, 1970), 35.
2. "Humblebrag." Oxford English Dictionary. https://www.lexico.com/en/definition/humblebrag.
3. Carson, *John*, 146.

ABOUT WHITE BLACKBIRD BOOKS

White blackbirds are extremely rare, but they are real. They are blackbirds that have turned white over the years as their feathers have come in and out over and over again. They are a redemptive picture of something you would never expect to see but that has slowly come into existence over time.

There is plenty of hurt and brokenness in the world. There is the hopelessness that comes in the midst of lost jobs, lost health, lost homes, lost marriages, lost children, lost parents, lost dreams, loss.

But there also are many white blackbirds. There are healed marriages, children who come home, friends who are reconciled. There are hurts healed, children fostered and adopted, communities restored. Some would call these events entirely natural, but really they are unexpected miracles.

The books in this series are not commentaries, nor

are they crammed with unique insights. Rather, they are a collage of biblical truth applied to current times and places. The authors share their poverty and trust the Lord to use their words to strengthen and encourage his people.

May this series help you in your quest to know Christ as he is found in the Gospel through the Scriptures. May you look for and even expect the rare white blackbirds of God's redemption through Christ in your midst. May you be thankful when you look down and see your feathers have turned. May you also rejoice when you see that others have been unexpectedly transformed by Jesus.

ALSO BY WHITE BLACKBIRD BOOKS

A Year in the New Testament: Volumes 1 & 2

All Are Welcome: Toward a Multi-Everything Church

The Almost Dancer

Birth of Joy: Philippians

Choosing a Church: A Biblical and Practical Guide

Christ in the Time of Corona: Stories of Faith, Hope, and Love

Co-Laborers, Co-Heirs: A Family Conversation

The Crossroads of Adultery

Doing God's Work

Driven by Desire

EmbRACE: A Biblical Study on Justice and Race

Ever Light and Dark: Telling Secrets, Telling the Truth

Everything Is Meaningless? Ecclesiastes

Faithful Doubt: Habakkuk

Firstfruits of a New Creation

Heal Us Emmanuel: A Call for Racial Reconciliation, Representation, and Unity in the Church

Hear Us, Emmanuel: Another Call for Racial Reconciliation, Representation, and Unity in the Church

In the Presence of Greatness: Isaiah

Insufficient: Pursuing Grace-Based Pastoral Competence

The Organized Pastor: Systems to Care for People Well

Questions of the Heart: Leaning In, Listening For, and Loving Well Toward True Identity in Christ

Rooted: The Apostles' Creed

A Sometimes Stumbling Life

Through the Valley: How Psalm 23 Helps in Suffering

To You I Lift Up My Soul: Confessions and Prayers

Urban Hinterlands: Planting the Gospel in Uncool Places

Follow whiteblackbirdbooks.pub for titles and releases.

ABOUT THE AUTHOR

John "Penny" Pennylegion is the Senior Pastor of Christ the King Presbyterian Church in Roanoke, Virginia. Penny has an MDiv and ThM from Covenant Theological Seminary where he also served as a visiting instructor of practical theology.

Penny can often be found watching good shows with his family, pulling for the St. Louis Cardinals, tackling the mountains of Southwest Virginia on his road bike, working in his yard, and cheering on his kids.

www.ingramcontent.com/pod-product-compliance
Lightning Source LLC
Chambersburg PA
CBHW071354090426
42738CB00012B/3119